Exeter and East Devon Dog Walks

Robert Hesketh

Bossiney Books • Exeter

All the walks in this book were checked prior to publication, at which time the instructions were correct. However, changes can occur in the countryside over which neither the author nor the publisher has any control. Please let us know if you encounter any serious problems.

The approximate locations of the walks in this book

South Devon Dog Walks

This companion book includes a number of walks in the Bovey Tracey–Newton Abbot–Teignmouth area.

First published 2023 by
Bossiney Books Ltd, 68 Thorndale Courts, Whitycombe Way,
Exeter, EX4 2NY,

www.bossineybooks.com

ISBN 978-1-915664-22-8

Acknowledgements

The maps are by Graham Hallowell,
except that on page 22 which is by Nick Hawkins
All photographs are by the author, www.roberthesketh.co.uk.

Printed in Great Britain by Deltor, Saltash, Cornwall

Introduction

These walks have been chosen with dogs in mind. All have off-lead opportunities; most have water for dogs to play in. I've avoided difficult stiles, unfenced cliffs and busy roads – many routes are off-road altogether. They range from a short run up to a half day's circuit of 8 km (5 miles), so the time needed to complete them will vary too.

The countryside

Walking is safe and healthy exercise for people and dogs, but beware of rising tides and strong currents. Devon rivers can rise fast and water that's normally safe for your dog can become hazardous after heavy rain. Please leave farm gates closed or open as you find them. Finally, please heed warning signs and keep your dog on a lead near livestock, especially during the lambing and bird nesting season. On Access Land, which includes the East Devon Commons and the Coastpath sections in this book, it is a legal requirement to keep your dog on a lead no more than 2 metres long between 1 March and 31 July and at all times around livestock.

Footwear and clothing

Walking is a pleasure throughout the seasons so long as you're prepared. Mud and puddles are par for the course. Devon's weather can change suddenly and it most certainly rains, so it's wise to take extra layers of clothing plus a waterproof. On some paths there may be gorse or nettles, so trousers are preferable to shorts, especially as they provide some protection against ticks which may carry debilitating Lyme disease and are intensely irritating. If a tick attaches itself to you or your dog, remove it promptly and carefully with tweezers – twist rather than pull.

Extras

Drinking water is a must for people and dogs. Very hot weather is best avoided, especially if your pet has a thick coat. I recommend walking poles or a stick too; a mobile phone and GPS device if you have them. The sketch maps in this book are just that – sketches. You may want to carry the relevant OS Explorer for extra information. Finally, please remember to take dog poo bags (preferably biodegradable) and dispose of them properly.

Thank you to all the kind dog owners and their dogs who agreed to be photographed for this book.

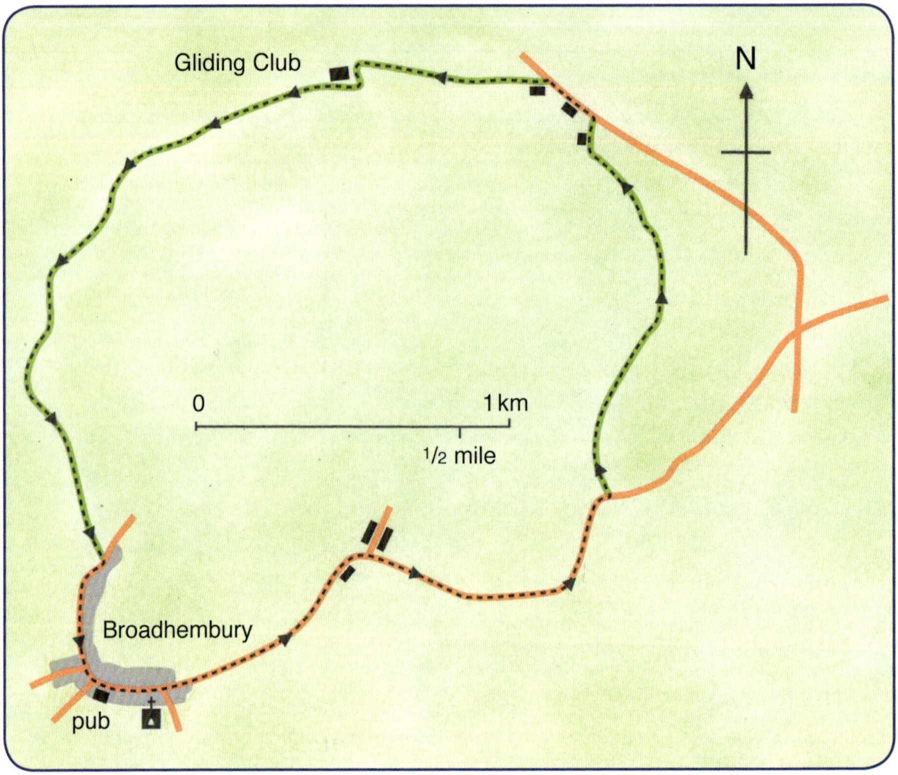

Walk 1 Broadhembury

Distance: 7.25 km (4 1/4 miles)
Character: Starting from Broadhembury, one of Devon's prettiest thatched villages, this walk climbs to 197 m (650 ft). There are fine views over the Blackdowns, the Otter Valley and Broadhembury itself. Parts of the route are off-lead, but please keep your dog leashed around livestock and when walking through the gliding club – where there's a good chance of seeing gliders and aircraft taking off and landing.

Park carefully in Broadhembury Square, ST 101048. Facing the war memorial, take the lane left uphill and follow it for 2 km (1 1/4 miles), following signs for DUNKESWELL AND SHELDON and ignoring side turnings. Be sure to keep right at Lane End Cross.

Turn left when the lane bends right after a stiff uphill section, into a PUBLIC BRIDLEWAY. Follow the bridleway for 1.2 km (3/4 mile) along the ridge, with trees on your left and fields on your right.

The bridleway turns sharp right. Follow it past farm buildings to a lane. Turn left along the lane for 120 m. Turn left again (PUBLIC BRIDLEWAY) at the entrance to the gliding club. Follow the beech lined drive ahead. Keep on the tarred track as you enter the gliding club and leash your dog.

Pause by a memorial bench, carved as a wyvern. Continue ahead as the drive becomes a grassy track. Follow the blue bridleway signs along the edge of the airfield – if the conditions are right, you may see gliders and light aircraft taking off and landing.

Keep to the bridleway as it bears left and downhill through trees and into a sunken track. Turn left over a stile, PUBLIC FOOTPATH. Cross a field to a second stile. Follow the clear path through a small wood. Cross a third stile and continue downhill as signed, over another stile into an enclosed path (please leash your dog) and on across fields by gates and stiles to meet a lane.

Turn right and follow the lane back to Broadhembury (as the lane bends left). Turn left over an arched bridge. Walk ahead to the square.

The Drewe Arms is on your right and Broadhembury's historic church straight ahead.

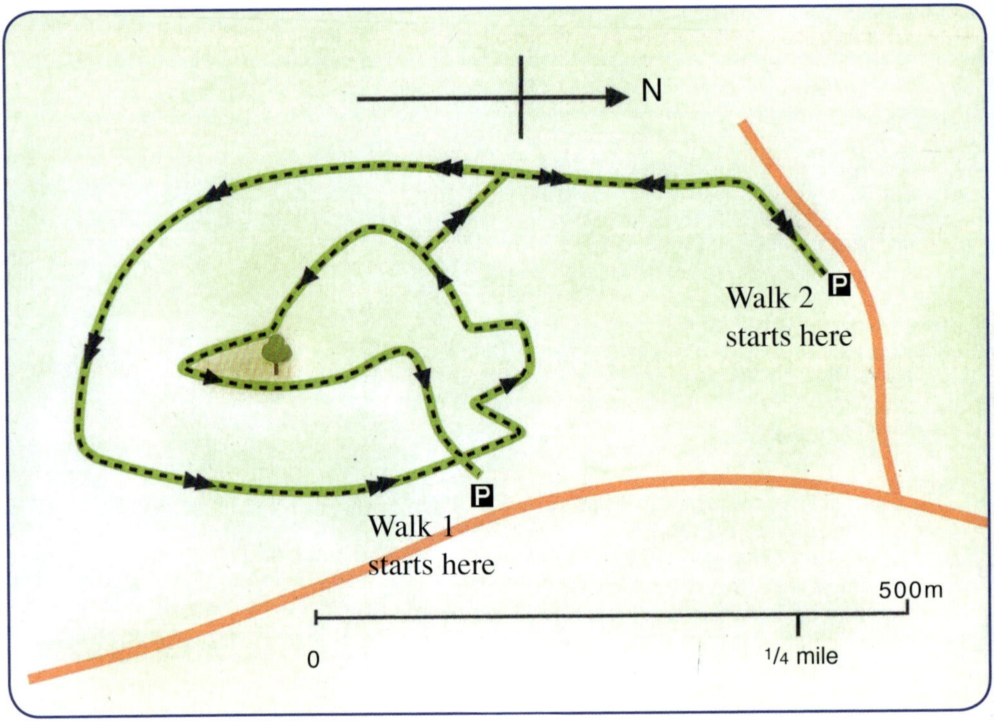

Walk 2 Dumpdon Hill

Distance: Walk One: 1.2km (3/4 mile). Walk Two: 3km (2 miles)

Character: Dumpdon Hill is an Iron Age hillfort with two ramparts and an internal area of 2.6ha. Standing 261m (861ft) above sea level, it gives wide ranging views. Walk One is a short ascent and tour of the ramparts. Walk Two explores the outer perimeter of the site as well. Please keep your dog leashed if livestock are present.

Getting there: turn left at Ford Cross, 3km (2miles) north-east of Honiton on the A30. Turn first left at Ford Bridge. Turn first right. Drive up steep Dumpdon Lane. Use the National Trust car park (ST178042) on the left for Walk One. Continue for 250m and turn left for the second NT car park (ST176045) for Walk Two.

Walk One: From the car park, climb the steps ahead. * Turn right, then left on the clear path. Turn right at the path junction, then left to the outer rampart. Turn left again, over the ditch to the inner rampart. Turn right and follow the inner rampart. Follow it when it turns left.

Head through a gate into a small beech wood. Walk ahead, then left around the perimeter of the wood. Leave by a gate (broken at the time of writing). Head along the inner rampart. Reaching a downhill path, turn right. Continue downhill to the car park.

Walk Two Follow the path ahead from the car park through trees. At the edge of the wood turn left and head steeply uphill. Turn right with a view of the ramparts on your left. Continue ahead around the fort.

This outer perimeter path meets the main path to the summit by a gate. To visit the fort itself as described in Walk One, turn to face the slope and follow the directions from point *. Leave through a gap on the northern edge of the ramparts. Turn right and retrace your steps to the start.

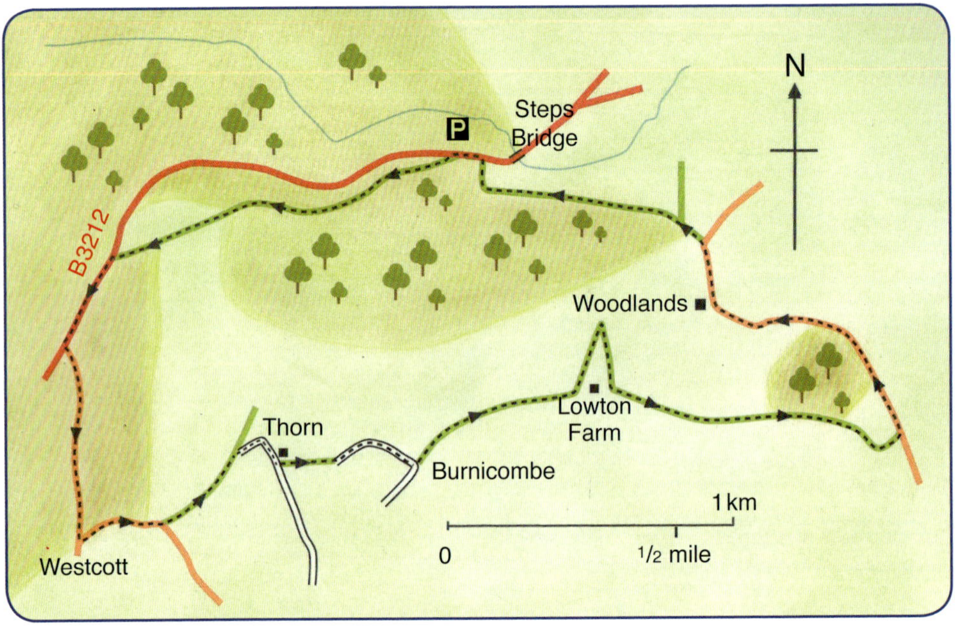

Walk 3 Bridford Wood and Steps Bridge

Distance: 7.7 km (4 3/4 miles)
Character: This route explores a beautiful but little visited corner of Devon. Much of it is off-lead and follows woodland and field paths, with short sections of quiet lanes and one 250 m section of quiet B road. It's quite an energetic walk, with several ascents and descents, compensated for by extensive views, wildflowers and birdsong.

Start from the signed car park on the north side of the B3212 just west of Steps Bridge. Use the information board to orient yourself. Cross the road and head uphill (PUBLIC BRIDLEWAY), initially on concrete. Continue through a gate.

Meeting the road, turn left and left again after 250 m, WESTCOTT. Follow the lane uphill. Follow the lane when it bends left and uphill. Turn left (PUBLIC FOOTPATH TO STEPS BRIDGE) over two stiles. Fine views open out. Reaching a tarred track, bear right and continue ahead. Ignore the footpath left, STEPS BRIDGE. Follow the lane right. Turn left (FOOTPATH BURNICOMBE FOR LOWTON) at Thorn Farm. Follow the well signed path along the field edge and over a stile. Continue down a track.

Bear left to Burnicombe. Turn right uphill for 50m. Turn left into the signed footpath and continue with the field edge on your left. Pass through a field gate. Continue along a fenced path. Follow the path when it turns left to Lowton. Bear left, TO PERMISSIVE BRIDLEWAY. Ignore the footpath immediately right. Continue downhill on the enclosed track.

Turn right, ALTERNATIVE PERMISSIVE BRIDLEWAY AVOIDING FARMYARD. Turn left (WINDMILL GATE) at a path junction and follow the clear path along field edges. Continue ahead over a stile and downhill with a wood on your left and field on your right.

Turn left down the lane. Follow on when the lane bends left, then right at Woodlands. When the lane bends right again continue ahead through a gate, BRIDLEWAY TO STEPS BRIDGE. Continue ahead at the path junction. Reaching the road, turn left to the start.

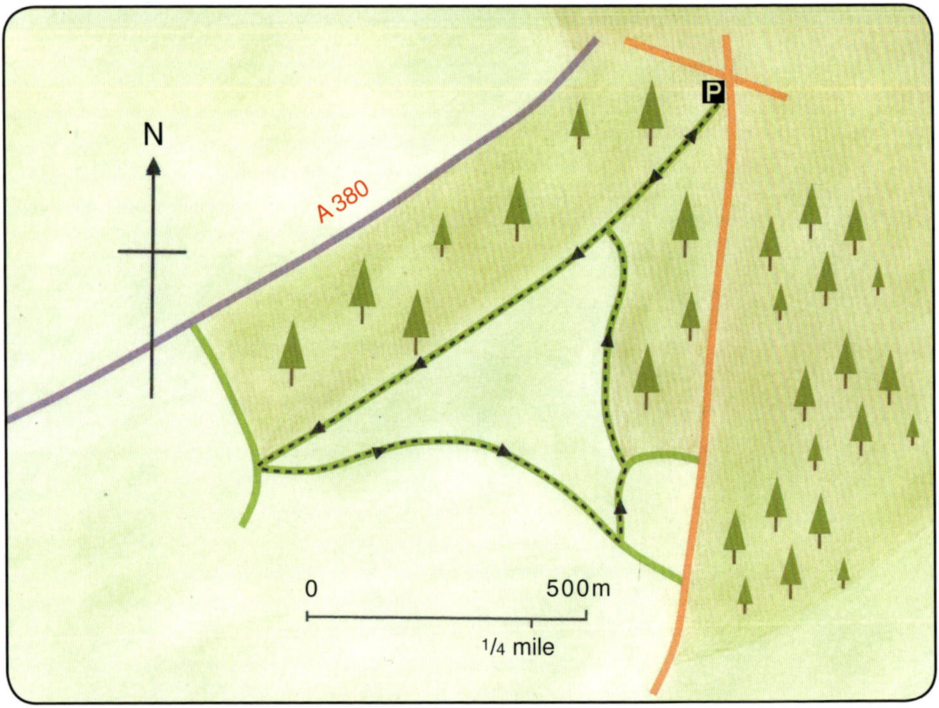

Walk 4 Ideford Common

Distance: 2.8km (1 3/4 miles)

Character: Ideford Common offers easy, largely level dog-friendly walking on well-defined and signed paths. Designated an SSSI (Site of Special Scientific Interest) because it is one of the last fragments of the heath that once covered much of the Haldon Hills, its specialised wildlife includes ground nesting birds such as skylarks and nightjars, so please keep your dog on a short lead from 1 March to 31 July. Enjoy superb views over the Teign Valley, rolling hills and patchwork fields to Dartmoor. Also of interest is a prehistoric barrow (tomb) in the north-east corner of the site and two small cairns located in the central northern part, close to the track.

Location: 200m down an unmarked lane on the west side of the B3192 (Teignmouth road) 500m south of Ashcombe Cross (A380) at SX903791.

Use the map and information board in the free car park to orientate yourself. Walk ahead on the broad path. Continue ahead at a cross-track along a clear, stony track, a bridleway.

Reaching a bridleway junction by a scrapyard, turn left as signed, following another clear track. Turn left at a bridleway waymark. Bear left at the next path junction and walk ahead across the heath. Turn right at the next path junction and retrace your steps to the start.

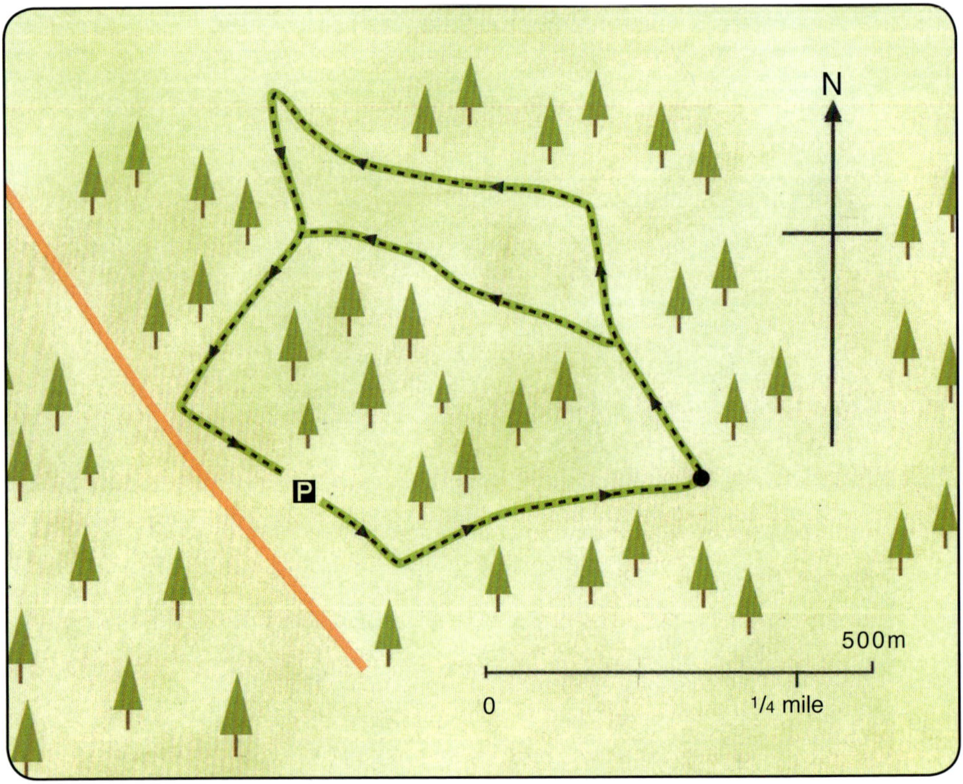

Walk 5 Mamhead

Distance: 1.4km (1 mile) or 1.8km (1 1/4 miles)

Character: Two well-signed, easy off-lead trails lead from Mamhead's large free car park through mixed woodland to a magnificent viewpoint looking out to the Exe estuary and the coast. The shorter trail is suitable for wheelchairs, being all level and well-surfaced. A longer loop extends the trail slightly, but includes some uneven track. Dog bins, benches and picnic tables are provided.

Getting there: From the A380 take the Mamhead/Starcross turning. Take the first right. Continue for 1km (1/2 mile), SX921808.

Take the path heading east from Mamhead's car park (NB not the path with the stone pillars). Pass a waymark, SHORT AND LONG LOOP. Continue to the viewpoint. Facing the viewpoint, turn left (SHORT AND LONG LOOP), heading north to a waymark. The path divides.

For the SHORT LOOP, turn left and continue ahead. Turn left again at the next waymark. Turn left again at the following waymark. Turn left once more at the third waymark and continue to the start.

For the LONG LOOP, walk ahead at the path division. Turn left at the next waymark and left again at the following waymark. Turn right at the next junction, SHORT AND LONG LOOPS. Continue ahead, then turn left at the waymark. Continue to the start.

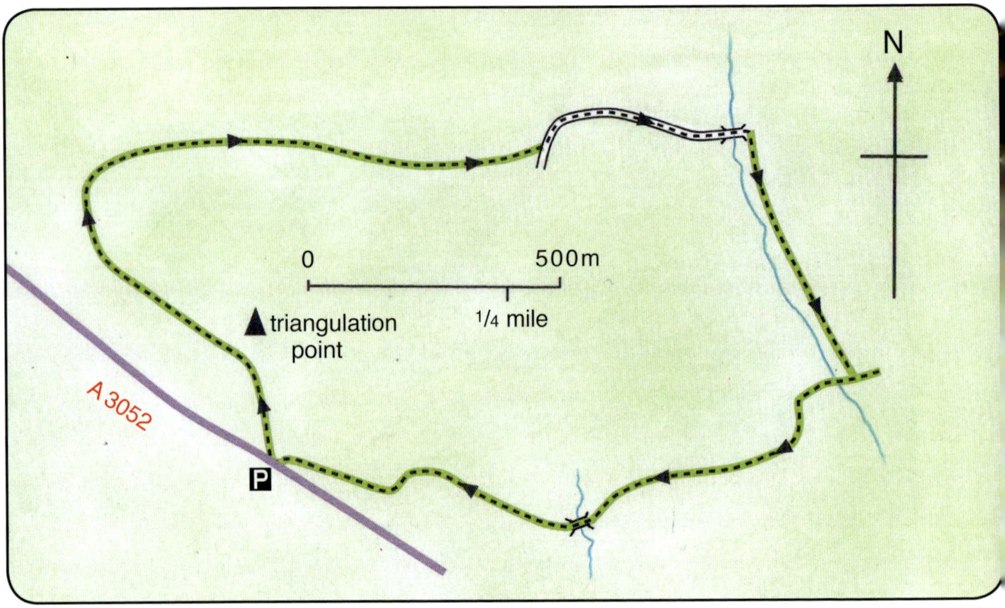

Walk 6 Harpford Hill and Aylesbeare Common

Distance : 4 km (2 1/2 miles)

Character: Aylesbeare Common is a 213 ha nature reserve on East Devon's pebblebed heaths and noted for its birds, plants and insects through the seasons. This walk follows a signed trail via ponds, streams, wet heathland and damp woodland edges. There are some moderate slopes. Please keep your dog under control and, from March to July, on a short leash to avoid disturbing wildlife.

Start from Joney's Cross car park on the south side of the A3052 at SY 057897, one mile west of NewtonPoppleford. Leave the car park and cross the road carefully. Walk ahead (EAST DEVON WAY) to the information board. Pick up a free leaflet and use the map to orient yourself.

Turn left and follow the broad path leading steadily away from the road. Bear left when you meet a path from the right near a triangulation pillar.

Continue ahead at the next junction by a waymark with a red circle. Continue on the path as it curves right (north). Reaching a cross-track, continue ahead at a waymark (yellow arrow). Follow this path as it veers east. Continue ahead at the next two waymarks.

Cross a tarred track and follow the path ahead. Divert left onto the tarred track by a cattle grid. Follow the tarred track downhill. It continues as a rough track, EAST DEVON WAY.

Cross a footbridge at the foot of the slope. Turn right and follow the path along the valley bottom with the stream on your right.

Turn right when you reach a cross-track by a field bank and waymark. Ford the brook and follow the path ahead. Continue as it curves left. Reaching a waymark and path junction, turn right and uphill. The path crosses a footbridge and continues uphill on the same course to the information board. Turn left here. Recross the road carefully and continue to the car park.

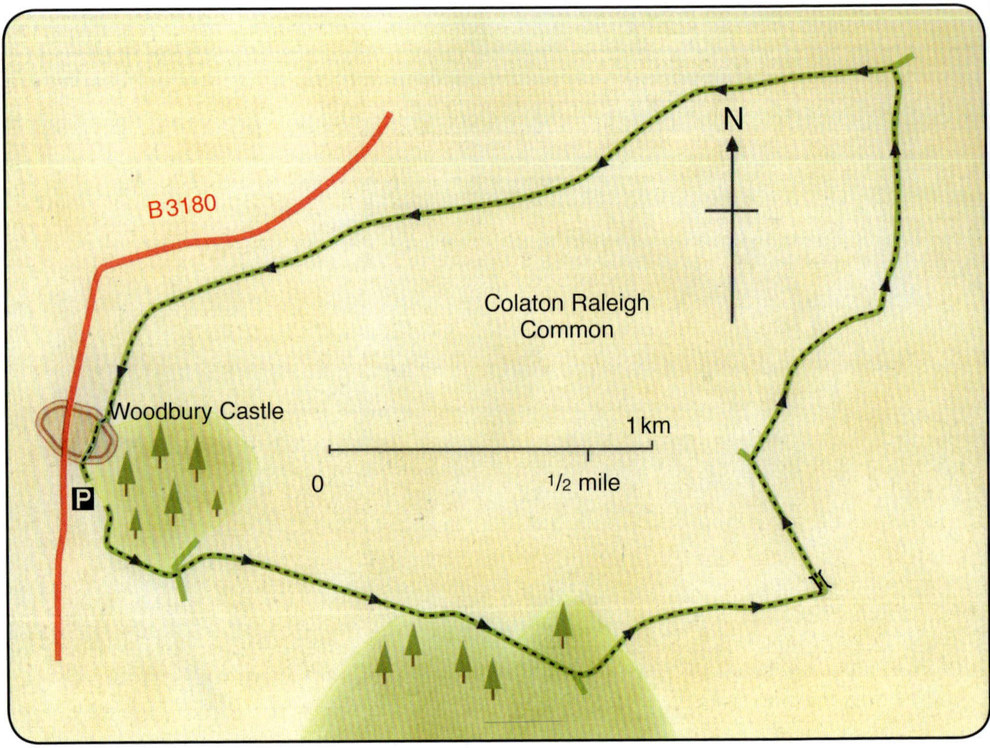

Walk 7 Woodbury Castle

Distance : *8 km (5 miles)*

Character: *The East Devon Commons, a mix of heath and mixed woodland, offer many miles of off-lead rambling (except during the bird-nesting season, March-July) and wide views over the patchwork green fields to the sea. This circuit of Colaton Raleigh Common from the Iron Age hillfort of Woodbury Castle is entirely off-road and follows signed tracks. There are ascents and descents, but nothing arduous. Attention to the directions is needed as the common is criss-crossed with paths and tracks, not all of which are shown in our sketch map, or on the Ordnance survy maps.*

Start from the car park on the eastern side of the B3180, SY033872. Take the path (pink arrow) from the northern end of the car park. At a waymark, turn right, then left onto a wide track leading east-south-east.

Continue ahead at a cross-track. Keep right at the next junction. Continue ahead at a blue waymark, ignoring tracks on your right and

left until you come to a waymark pointing left at a clear track division.

Turn left here. Continue ahead and follow the bridlepath ahead then downhill as signed, right to the bottom of the slope, where the path divides. Turn left and cross a footbridge.

Follow the track ahead. Continue uphill at blue waymarks until you reach a path division with a waymark signed FIRE POINT 17. Turn right here and follow the bridlepath north-east. When the path divides, turn left at a blue waymark. Just 25 m ahead, keep right at a second waymark. At the next junction, turn left, PUBLIC BRIDLEWAY.

Reaching another path junction, turn left at the waymark. Follow the blue and pink waymarks ahead on a westerly course. Keep left at a path junction as the track veers to the south-west at a pink waymark.

Continue ahead. When the track divides, continue ahead. The path divides again at the next waymark. Keep left, veering south towards Woodbury Castle, which is hidden among trees.

The track divides. Keep right, then turn left and follow the path ahead, parallel to the outer rampart. Turn right, down and up steps, to enter the castle. A display board explains its history. Leave by steps at the south-western corner. Continue to the car park.

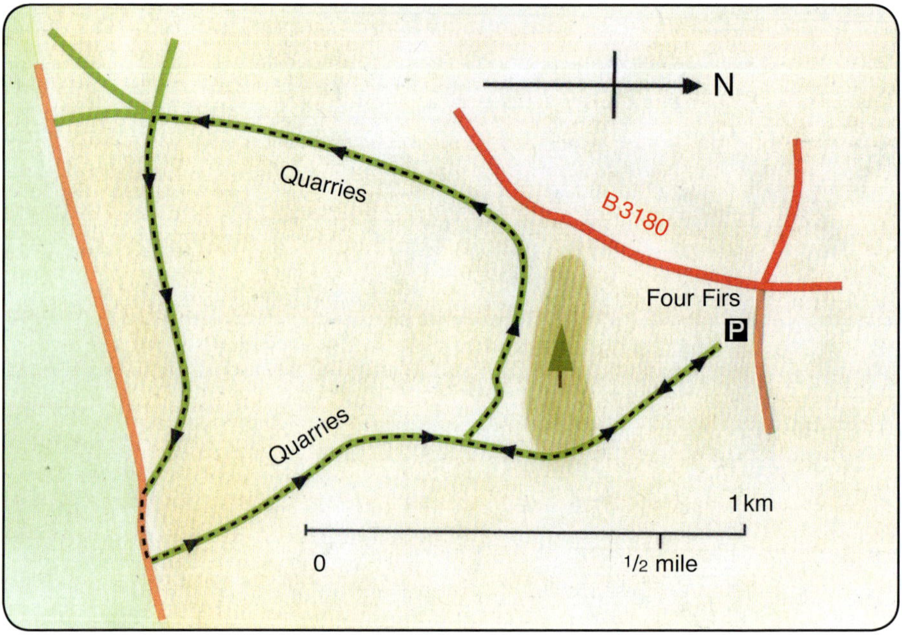

Walk 8 Bicton Common

Distance : 4.5 km (2 3/4 miles)

Character : Like the Woodbury Castle walk (page 16), this route explores East Devon's pebblebed heaths, a pleasing mix of heath and woodland with wide views to the sea. Much of the walk is off-lead, but please stay on the paths and do not allow your dog into the fenced former quarries, for its own safety and to protect ground-nesting birds. There are some short ascents and descents, but nothing arduous.

Start from the signed Four Firs car park on the eastern side of the B3180 at SY032864. Take the path signed EAST DEVON WAY. Branch left at the pink waymark, EAST DEVON WAY. Continue ahead at a cross-track.

Continue past a stand of conifers down a steep slope. Near the bottom of the slope, turn very sharp right (PUBLIC BRIDLEWAY) at a waymark and follow this path through the heath.

Reaching a path near the road, leash your dog and turn left through a gate. Turn left again onto a tarred track, PUBLIC BRIDLEWAY. Follow it uphill. Continue ahead, PUBLIC BRIDLEWAY. When the path divides, continue ahead to a bridleway cross-track.

Turn left, PUBLIC BRIDLEWAY. Continue ahead at the crosstracks and keep the same course, ignoring side turnings. When in doubt, keep right. Reaching a lane, leash your dog and turn left.

Turn left again, PUBLIC BRIDLEWAY. Follow the broad track ahead. Meeting the bridlepath you branched off on earlier in the walk, continue ahead (pink arrow), retracing your steps to the start.

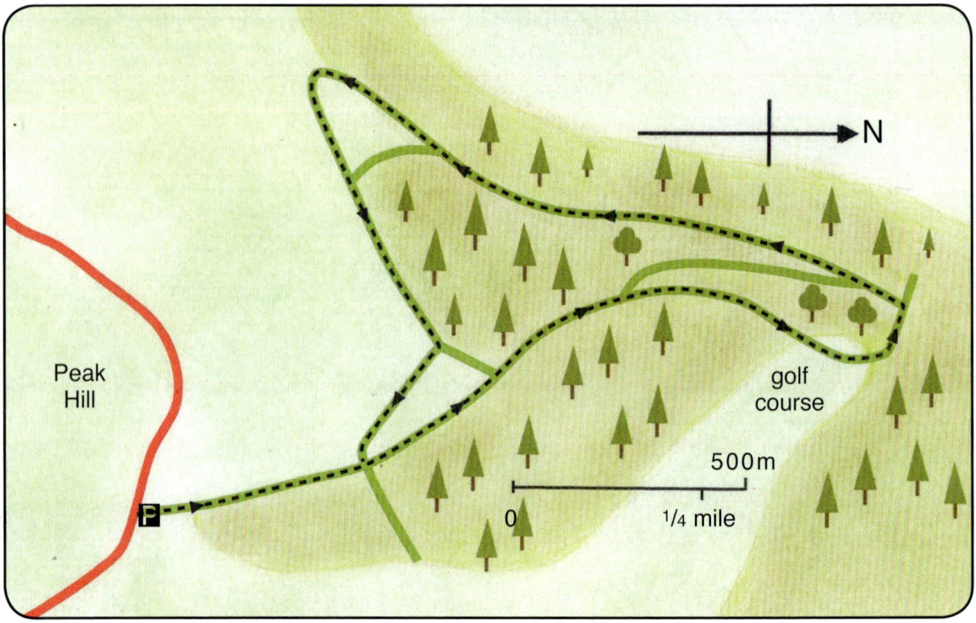

Walk 9   Mutters Moor

Distance: 4.6 km (3 miles)

Character: Mutters Moor is an attractive blend of mixed woodland and heath, crisscrossed by paths and forestry tracks. Largely level, with a few short slopes, it is great for off-lead walks – apart from in the bird nesting season (1 March -31 July) and a short path over the golf course.

Mutter is a Devon surname and Abe Mutter, an associate of the notorious Beer smuggler Jack Rattenbury, owned land on Mutters Moor. This and his turf-cutting business on the moor provided useful concealment for contraband during the classic smuggling era of the 18th and early 19th centuries.

Start from the car park towards the top of Peak Hill on the steep road climbing out of Sidmouth. Use the map and notice board near the lower entrance to orient yourself, and take the broad track ahead. Continue ahead at a path junction and at the following junction. Ignore the path joining from the left and the broad track on the left. When the track forks, keep right (PUBLIC BRIDLEWAY) and head into mixed woodland. Leash your dog as you cross the golf course. Enjoy a fine view to the sea.

Turn left at the far side of the golf course. Follow the track uphill to a cross-track. Turn left (PUBLIC BRIDLEWAY) heading south-west. The track soon divides. Walk ahead, PUBLIC BRIDLEWAY PEAK HILL. Fine views can be glimpsed through the trees. Ignore a series of tracks on the left.

Keep left at a path junction and follow the track as it curves left. When the track divides keep ahead, PUBLIC BRIDLEWAY. Meeting a track from the left, keep right and right again at the fingerpost, PUBLIC BRIDLEWAY SEVEN STONES. Turn left only 20m ahead. Continue on the path ahead, ignoring side turnings to join the track on which you first set out. Turn right and retrace your steps to the start.

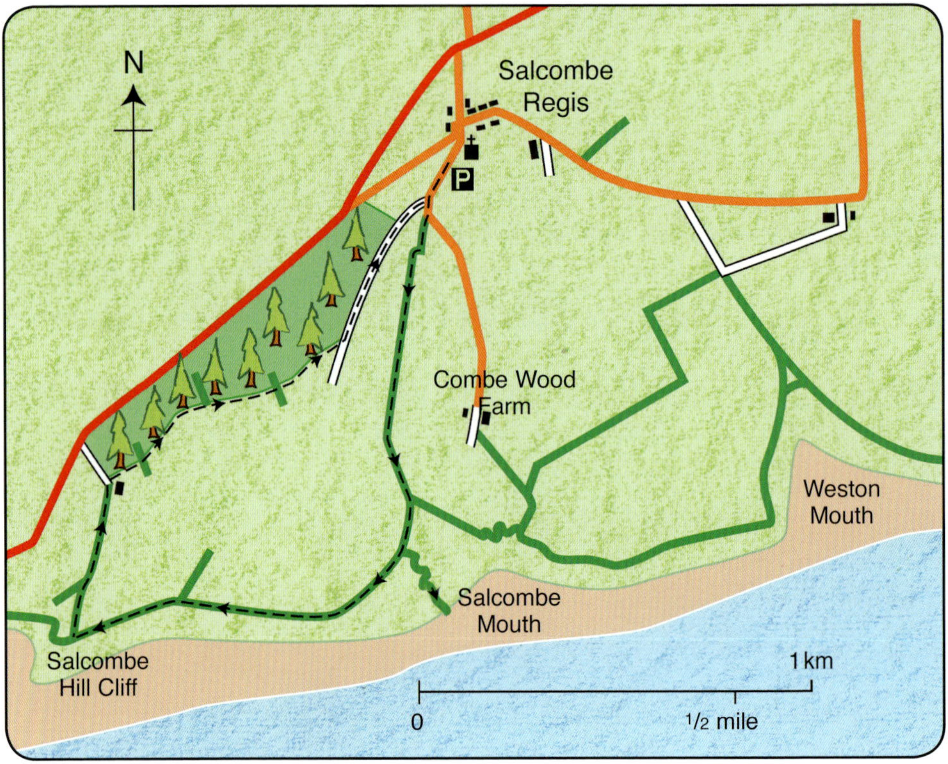

Walk 10 Salcombe Regis

Distance: 3.9 km (2 1/2 miles)

Character: This demanding, but very rewarding walk includes Salcombe Mouth, a large dog-friendly pebble beach, which is never crowded. The views east to Portland Bill and west to Torbay from both Salcombe Mouth and Salcombe Hill Cliff are stunning. There is a long flight of steps to the beach and a steep walk to the top of the cliff, but the path is fenced. Please leash your dog if livestock are present.

Start from Salcombe Regis church car park (contributions requested, SY 148888). Turn left down the lane. Ignore the first footpath right, take the second, 30 m ahead, PUBLIC FOOTPATH SALCOMBE MOUTH AND COAST PATH.

Follow this path downhill through fields and gates to a bridge and fingerpost. Continue ahead, COAST PATH SALCOMBE MOUTH SIDMOUTH. Divert left down the steep, stepped path as signed to Salcombe Mouth.

Return to the Coastpath. At first, it rises gently over the sandstone, but the gradient increases sharply when it reaches the greensand, chalk and flints which cap the cliff. Rest on the bench half-way up and look east to Higher Dunscombe Cliff, a similar formation with the reddish sandstone at the base and the creamy coloured greensand above.

A second bench stands at the summit of Salcombe Hill Cliff, 164 m (541 ft) above the sea. Ignore the footpath right and continue on the Coast Path to the next fingerpost. Turn right, SALCOMBE HILL CAR PARK – but before you do, walk ahead 50 m to the viewing table. Sidmouth lies below, with the New Red Sandstone cliffs beyond. The first of these is High Peak, an impressive 157 m (518 ft).

Continue ahead at the next path junction, PUBLIC FOOTPATH. Only 50 m ahead, turn right in front of the drive gate and follow the footpath through trees. This path continues along the edge of the plantation to a path junction. Continue ahead (SALCOMBE REGIS), following the woodland path steeply downhill to a track. Again, continue ahead, PUBLIC FOOTPATH. Reaching the tarred lane, turn left. The car park is 100 m further on.

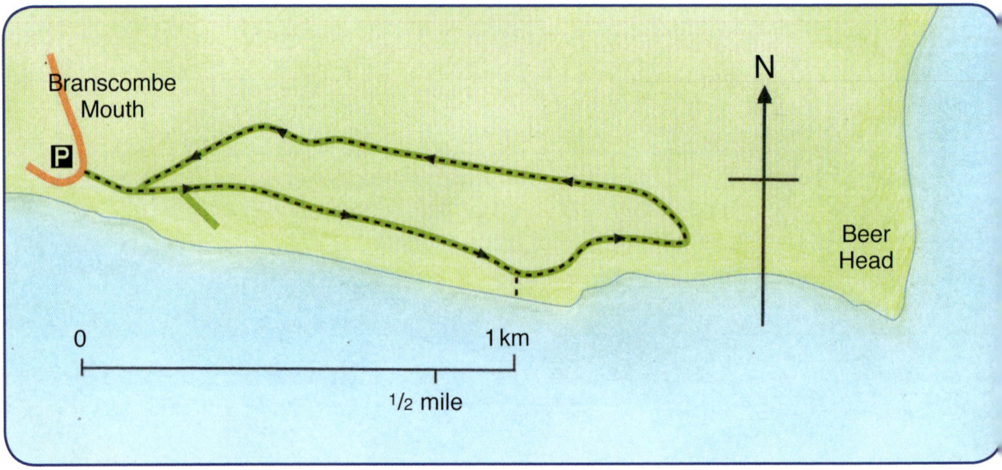

Walk 11 Branscombe

Distance : 3.8 km (2½ miles)

Character: This exhilarating coastal walk has magnificent views, a dog-friendly beach with two access points and off-lead walking on both the undercliff path and (unless livestock are present) the contrasting clifftop path. There is a tough ascent and descent.

Start from Branscombe Mouth car park, with its café and toilets. Take the COAST PATH BEER and start climbing. Bear right on the lower path (COAST PATH BEER) at a junction and fingerpost. Fork left at a path division and continue past chalets. Continue ahead (COAST PATH BEER) into the undercliff path.

Turn right on to a short path leading to the beach, a diversion which

The geology of Hooken Undercliff is fascinating: like the more extensive undercliffs between Lyme Regis and Axmouth (page 30), it was created by landslip and its vegetation and micro-climate are quite different from the clifftop. One night in 1790, heavy rain caused the top layer of chalk and greensand to slide over the layer of clay which separated it from the limestone (lias) below. Four hectares of land slipped 60 m down and 200 m seaward, creating what we see today.

gives access to a huge stretch of pebble bank with magnificent views and no dog restrictions. Return to the Coast Path and continue east. Follow it up as it zigzags to the top of the cliff.

Reaching the top, turn left, PUBLIC FOOTPATH BRANSCOMBE. The clifftop path is fenced, but please leash your dog if livestock are present. The path is fairly level, before descending steeply. Divert to Branscombe beach, where dogs are permitted in a 300 m wide zone.

Walk 12 Brampford Speke and Stoke Canon

The Exe Valley Way provides pleasant riverside walking by foot- and field-paths, but please keep your dog on a lead near livestock.

If starting from Brampford Speke, park carefully in the main street. Head north past the church and pub. Turn right at the school sign. Follow the lane right, then left and downhill to an arched bridge.* Turn left and follow the signed path. When it divides, keep right on the fenced path. The best swimming spots are 750 m upriver.

Starting from Stoke Canon, park carefully near the church. Walk down the main street to the post office. Turn right into CHESNUT CRESCENT. Continue over the level crossing. Turn almost immediately left through a gate, PUBLIC FOOTPATH. This follows the bed of the dismantled railway and bends right. Leaving the railway, the footpath crosses a small bridge and continues to a larger arched bridge. From there, follow the directions from * above.

Walk 13 Stoke Woods

Although only two miles from the centre of Exeter, Stoke Woods feels surprisingly remote. A labyrinth of paths criss-cross this ancient woodland, designated an SSSI for its wildlife value. All are suitable for off-lead walking, but please remember the A396 passes below the woods and Pennsylvania Road above. There is a small car park on the A396 at SX919959 and another on Pennsylvania Road at SX924958.

Walk 14 Exe Estuary Trail West

The western half of the Exe Estuary Trail offers a delightful traffic-free route out of the city beside the Exeter Canal. There are several possible starting points, the most obvious being Exeter's picturesque quay. From there, follow the towpath south for 750 m (1/2 mile) to Trew's Weir. For a longer walk, continue to Countess Weir (3.5 km/ 2 1/4 miles); the Topsham Foot Ferry (6 km/3 3/4 miles) or Turf Locks and Hotel (7.5 km/4 3/4 miles), where the canal joins the river Exe.

Another good starting point with direct access to the trail is the car park on Exminster Marshes at SX964873, only 1.25 km (3/4 mile) from Turf Locks. Parts of this popular route are shared with cyclists, so please keep your dog under control.

Walk 15 Little Haldon

Little Haldon has two short off-lead walks. The National Trust car park on the eastern side of the B3192 5km (3 miles) north of Teignmouth at SX918765 (dog bin provided) opens onto 18ha of heath with several paths to explore and fine views out to sea. Postman's Path lies 1.6km (1 mile) south. Park either at Postman's Path car park, SX920750, near the northern end of Shepherd's Lane or at White Wells car park and picnic area (dog bin provided), SX 919750 at the southern end of Teignmouth Golf Course. Postman's Path is a 750 m long public footpath joining the two car parks. Enjoy great views of the Teign estuary.

Walk 16 Exe Estuary Trail, East

The Exe Estuary Trail is a 42 km (26 mile) long cycle- and walk-way, linked on the eastern bank by the Avocet Line. This delightful dog-friendly branch railway (dogs travel free) connects Exeter and Exmouth. It has eleven stations, four of which – Topsham, Exton, Lympstone and Exmouth – are on the trail, making good starting points for linear walks. These points also have convenient parking.

From Exeter, the best starting points are Exeter Quay and the Swing Bridge. Whilst some sections are dedicated footpath, others are shared with cyclists. Please keep your dog under control.

Walk 17 Budleigh Salterton to Otterton

There's fine riverside walking beside the river Otter between Budleigh Salterton and Ottery St Mary, but the 3.6 km (2 1/2 mile) path between Budleigh and Otterton is deservedly the most popular. Start by the entrance to Budleigh's Lime Kiln car park and take PUBLIC FOOTPATH away from the beach. (East of this point, dogs are permitted on the pebbly beach all year; west of it dogs are only permitted between October and April).

Follow the path behind the car park and left along the edge of the salt marshes. The marshes (once salt pans) are a Devon Wildlife Trust reserve noted for ducks, geese and waders. Please keep your dog leashed here and upriver, where beavers have been re-introduced. The path, level and largely well-surfaced, follows the river to Otterton, with its working watermill, which has a gallery, shops, bakery and café besides.

Walk 18 Colyton riverbank walk

From Colyton there is a delightful 3.5 km (2 1/4 mile) walk beside the river Coly. It passes through green fields and is suitable for off-lead walking where livestock are not present. Leave your car in Colyton's main car park. Walk ahead across the square and along a footpath beside the churchyard. Turn left opposite the iron gates. Follow VICARAGE STREET ahead to a T junction. Turn right over the bridge. Turn left (EAST DEVON WAY) onto the riverbank path.

Walk 19 Lyme Regis Undercliffs

Start from Holmbush car park on the western edge of Lyme Regis, SY 336920. Follow the PUBLIC FOOTPATH at the southern end of the car park to a path junction. Continue on the COAST PATH. Keep right (east) at the next junction and into the 304 ha Axmouth-Lyme Regis Nature Reserve. An information board explains how landslips have created the undercliffs, where a variety of plants and animals thrive.

Continue ahead for 1.5 km through dense woodland along the fairly level but uneven Coast Path to get a flavour of the undercliffs, eerily quiet apart from birdsong and the murmur of insects.

Alternatively, branch right at the second information panel and climb steeply to Chimney Rock for an overview of the undercliffs – though dense foliage obscures this in summer.

Haldon Forest

Haldon Forest has three well marked walking trails with dog bins and benches. They are themed to help visitors appreciate different aspects of Haldon Forest and start from Haldon Forest Gateway car park, SX884849, where facilities include a café and toilets. Use the map and information board at the car park to orient yourself, pick up a map from the information desk or download the information from the Haldon Forest website.

The 2.5km (1 1/2 mile) Discovery Trail is fully surfaced and suitable for wheelchairs and buggies. Also fully surfaced, the Raptor Trail (4.5km/3 miles) has some steep slopes, whilst the Butterfly Trail (6km/4 miles) has varied surfaces. However, they are all suitable for trampers. All are off-lead, but multi-use: watch out for cyclists and other users.

Ashclyst Forest

Ashclyst Forest's 300 ha of mixed woodland is criss-crossed by footpaths and served by several car parks, the most central being Forest Gate, SX999994. Use the helpful map and information boards there to orient yourself and choose one of the clearly signed walks. These range from the 20 minute yellow route (suitable for buggies), to the blue, green and red routes (30, 45 and 60 minutes respectively). Designed to show the forest's history, tree species and wildlife, which includes Ashclyst's nationally important butterfly populations, all are off-lead, but the National Trust asks walkers to keep their dogs under control and in sight at all times.

Some of the best dog friendly beaches in East Devon

East Devon has an array of dog friendly beaches, though most have some (mainly seasonal) restrictions. Among the best are Dawlish Warren, Salcombe Mouth (page 22), Exmouth (page 28), Budleigh Salterton (page 29), Weston Mouth (page 22) and Branscombe (page 24).

Full details of these and other dog friendly beaches are given in my *Devon Beach and Cove Guide*.